castles

Written by
FRANCESCA BAINES

Illustrated by
MARK BERGIN

Series Created & Designed by
DAVID SALARIYA

WATTS BOOKS
London • New York • Sydney

CONTENTS

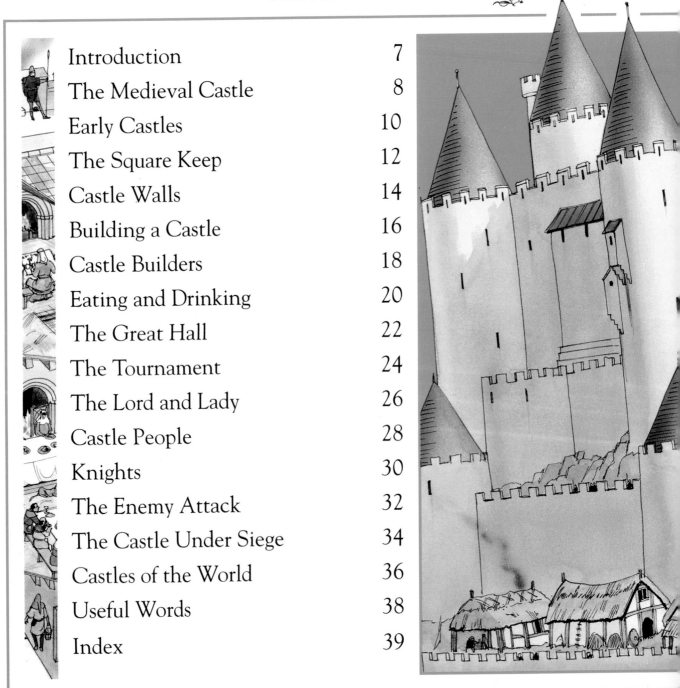

**This book is to be returned on or before
the last date stamped below.**

LIBREX

SERIES EDITOR   DAVID SALARIYA
EDITOR   RUTH NASON
EDITORIAL ASSISTANT   APRIL McCROSKIE

Published in 1995
by Watts
WATTS 96 Leonard Street
London EC2A 4RH
This edition 1997

ISBN 0 7496 1657 1
Dewey Classification 728.8

© THE SALARIYA BOOK COMPANY LTD MCMXCV

Printed in Belgium

A CIP catalogue record for this book is available from the British Library.

A castle was a fortress built for protection against enemy armies. But it was the home of a lord and his followers too. It also protected the people who worked on the castle lands and lived in the villages nearby. Over the centuries a castle often had to be strengthened many times. This was because weapons became more and more powerful. Castles were most important between the 11th and 15th centuries, during a period called the Middle Ages. On the next page you will see a castle from the 14th century.

THE MEDIEVAL CASTLE

The Middle Ages was the period between the 5th and the 15th centuries.

The 11th century was from 1000 to 1099.

The 12th century was from 1100 to 1199.

The 13th century was from 1200 to 1299.

The 14th century was from 1300 to 1399.

The 15th century was from 1400 to 1499.

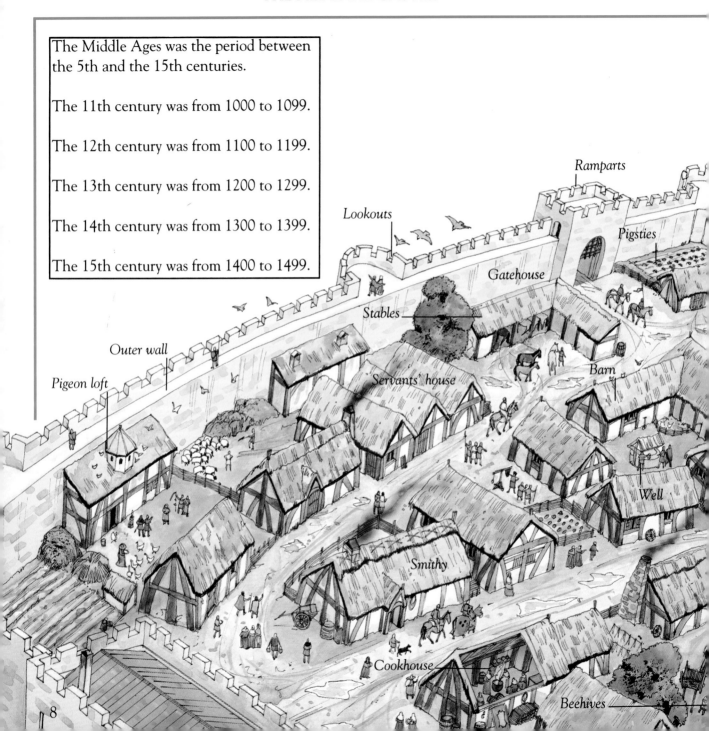

Lookouts

Ramparts

Pigsties

Gatehouse

Stables

Outer wall

Servants' house

Barn

Pigeon loft

Well

Smithy

Cookhouse

Beehives

8

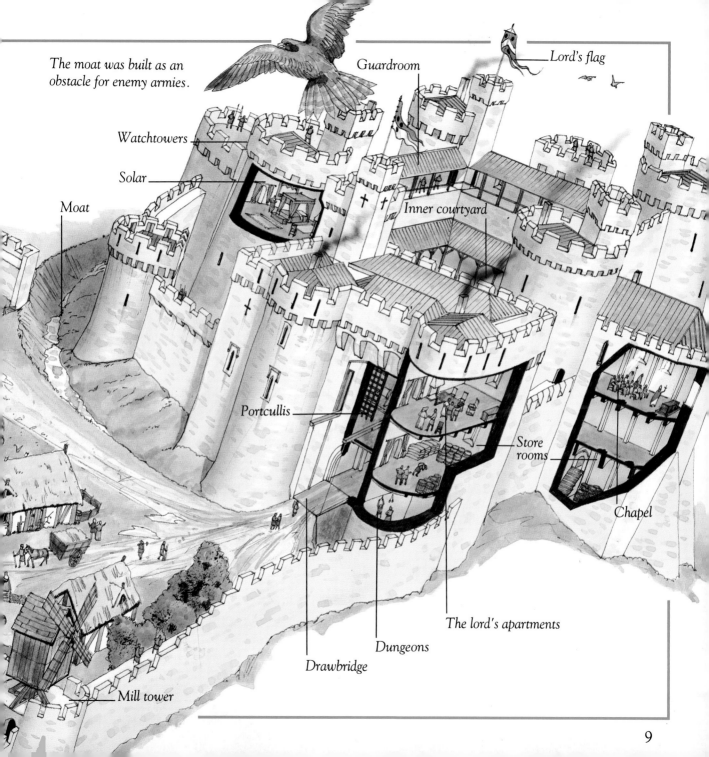

The moat was built as an obstacle for enemy armies.

Guardroom

Lord's flag

Watchtowers

Solar

Moat

Inner courtyard

Portcullis

Store rooms

Chapel

Drawbridge

Dungeons

The lord's apartments

Mill tower

9

The Norman army conquered new lands and quickly built castles to defend their position. The castles were made of wood and earth. Some took only one day to build. Many were rebuilt later using stone. This took many years, but made the castles much stronger.

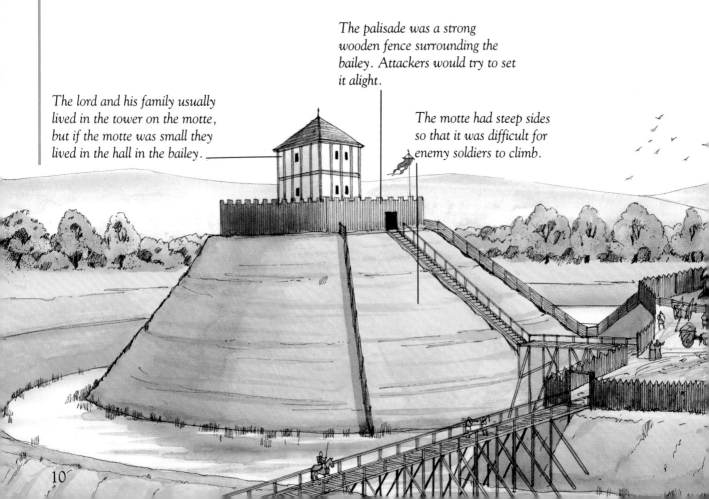

The palisade was a strong wooden fence surrounding the bailey. Attackers would try to set it alight.

The lord and his family usually lived in the tower on the motte, but if the motte was small they lived in the hall in the bailey.

The motte had steep sides so that it was difficult for enemy soldiers to climb.

Some of the first castles

were made of wood. The wooden tower was built on a mound of earth, called a motte. At the foot of the mound there was a fenced yard, called a bailey. These castles were built in the 11th and 12th centuries and were the homes of rulers called lords. The lord could be a king or a nobleman, and he lived in the castle with his servants and followers.

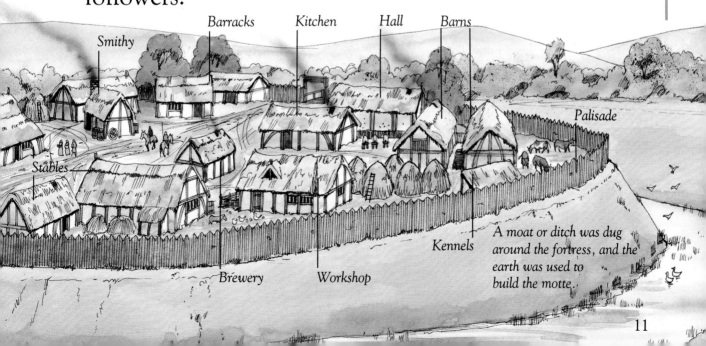

Smithy

Barracks

Kitchen

Hall

Barns

Palisade

Stables

Kennels

Brewery

Workshop

A moat or ditch was dug around the fortress, and the earth was used to build the motte.

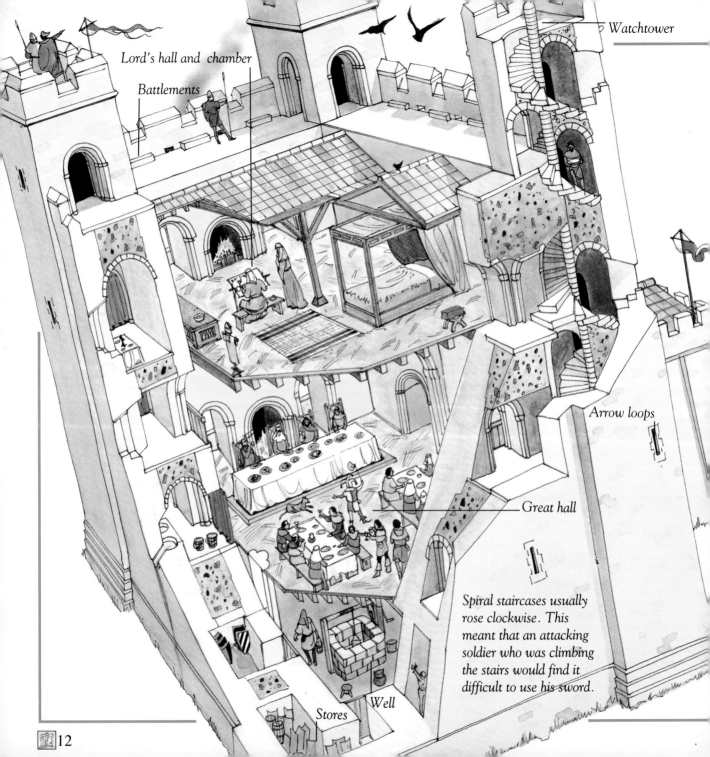

Watchtower

Lord's hall and chamber

Battlements

Arrow loops

Great hall

Spiral staircases usually rose clockwise. This meant that an attacking soldier who was climbing the stairs would find it difficult to use his sword.

Stores

Well

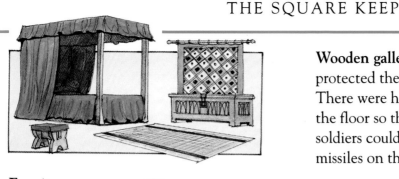

Wooden galleries protected the soldiers. There were holes in the floor so that the soldiers could drop missiles on the enemy.

Furniture was made so that the lord could take it with him from castle to castle, even the four-poster bed.

The enemy would attack the keep by tunnelling under the castle.

Stronger castles were needed as weapons became more powerful. Many lords replaced the wooden tower with a square, stone building called a keep. It had a tower at each corner. Then a thick stone wall was built around the keep, which made it almost impossible for the enemy to get in.

Inner wall

Moat

Outer wall

14

An outer wall was added to many castles

in the 13th century. It was lower than the inside wall so that several rows of soldiers could shoot arrows at the same time. The keep was the safest place in an attack, but people preferred to live in houses in the courtyard, or in rooms in the walls. The best way to capture these castles was to surround them until people surrendered from hunger or thirst. This was called a siege. On the next page you can see inside a castle keep.

Outer courtyard

Gatehouse

A fair

The barbican protected the outer gate.

Drawbridge

15

Workmen were supervised by a master mason. He was helped by a clerk who did the accounts and bought the materials. The stone was bought in rough blocks and then shaped and carved by skilled masons.

Master mason   Clerk   Stone-porters   Masons

Building a castle needed hundreds of craftsmen and skilled workers who were helped by gangs of unskilled labourers. If the castle had to be finished quickly, soldiers, farmhands and even prisoners would have to help with the building. All these workers were organised into teams led by a master craftsman.

Stone masons cut the stones so they fitted together exactly.

Blacksmiths made nails.

Carpenters made roofs and beams.

Plumbers poured molten lead into frames to make sheets for the roof.

Glass-blower

Glaziers made windows.

Some machines helped with the building of a castle. This winch attached to a treadmill was for lifting heavy things.

Stone was brought from local quarries.

Castle walls were very thick. Two walls were built and the centre was filled with flint and rubble.

Many of the tools used in the Middle Ages, such as trowels and chisels, are still used in building today.

The site of a castle was carefully chosen. It was built in a place that was difficult to attack, like the edge of a cliff, or on a hill.

Mortar was a mixture of sand, quicklime and water. It was used to bond the stones together.

Scaffolding was made from wooden poles held in place with ropes.

Grape press

Ovens

Spit

Cauldron

Firewood came from the lord's forests.

The kitchen was usually in a separate building, or outside in the courtyard, because of the risk of fire. It was always busy with people preparing meals and preserving food. Meat was roasted over the fire on a spit. Other food was usually cooked in a big pot called a cauldron.

Butler

The brewer made the castle beer.

Beer

Fresh meat

Every drop of water used had to be drawn from the well.

Bread was baked each day in brick ovens. Drink was made in the kitchen, too. The brewer made beer, and some castles had a grape press for making wine. Good stores of food and drink were vital for the people of the castle if there was a siege.

Fresh meat could be salted or pickled to preserve it.

Slices of stale bread, called trenchers, were used as plates. Later they were given to the poor as food.

Tapestries were used to decorate the walls.

Only the lord's family and guests sat on chairs, at a separate table. The rest of the household sat on benches.

People cut food with knives but they had no forks. They ate using their fingers.

Minstrels sang and played music to entertain people as they ate.

Pages brought food from the kitchen.

Dogs would finish up any scraps.

Herbs were often scattered on the ground so the hall would smell good.

Jugglers and acrobats would travel from castle to castle performing their acts.

Beer was drunk with every meal, even breakfast, as the water was sometimes bad.

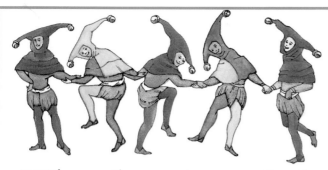

Fools or jesters had to make people laugh. They did this with their comic dances, funny poems and tales.

The heart of the castle was the great hall. Here people would gather to eat, do business and have fun. At night the tables and benches were folded away and household servants laid straw mattresses around the fire to sleep on. The fire was often in the middle of the hall but a high ceiling stopped the room from getting too smoky.

Mummers would sometimes call at the castle. They were local people in disguise, and they danced or performed plays in exchange for food, drink or money. It was considered very unlucky to send them away.

23

The lord of the castle was responsible for managing his lands and for local law and order. He was often an important figure in the army, too. This meant he sometimes had to go away to fight for his country, or in the Crusades. While he was away his lady would take command. For pleasure, the lord and lady would go hunting. They also liked to watch their knights jousting in tournaments, like the one shown on the previous page.

Richly-coloured clothes were the fashion in the Middle Ages. By law, only the nobility could wear very fine clothes.

A lord often had several castles on his lands and he would stay at each one in turn. Wherever he went a large group of his followers and servants travelled with him.

Castle gardens were usually enclosed by a hedge or a fence. They were used for growing food, but were also full of flowers and trees planted in beautiful patterns for the lord and lady to enjoy.

Hunting was a popular sport for both lords and ladies. They hunted for deer, wild boar, foxes, wolves, otters, hares and rabbits.

A spiked collar protected dogs from a boar's tusks.

27

CASTLE PEOPLE

Peasants had a very hard life. They had to work on the lord's fields, as well as their own, in exchange for living on his land.

Soldiers practised their skills with a lance by aiming at a wooden shield called a quintain.

Inside the castle wall it was like a small village. If there was an attack, the people would go into the castle for protection.

The roof was made of thatched reeds or straw.

Houses had timber frames and walls of woven twigs, mud and straw.

The whole family worked, cooked and slept in just one room.

Gardens were important for growing food.

The villagers all worked together to plant the corn in the autumn. Animals could help with some of the work, but most jobs were done by hand.

Driving oxen

Breaking up the soil

Bird-scaring

Ploughing

Harrowing

Sowing seed

Marshal

The lord's family　　　*Chaplain*　*Clerks*

Many people helped the lord and lady to run the castle. The marshal decided who lived in which rooms. The chaplain held services in the private chapel. Clerks kept the castle accounts.

All kinds of people worked in a castle.

They served the lord and his family, and helped manage their affairs. Other people were needed to make many of the things that were used in the castle, like cloth, furniture and even armour. Peasants worked on the castle lands. They lived in the villages nearby.

Archers were soldiers who used a bow and arrow. Crossbowmen used a crossbow. The butler and pantler looked after food, drink and stores. The bailiff collected the lord's rent.

Pages worked for the knights and helped serve at meals. Grooms worked in the stables and cared for the horses. The reeve managed the lord's farms.

Archer　*Knights*　*Maidservant*
　　　　　　Bailiff　*Pantler*
Crossbowman　　　　　　*Butler*

Cook　*Pages*　*Reeve*
Kitchen workers　*Grooms*　*Spinner*

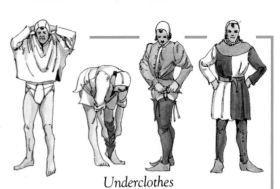

Armour protected a knight from heavy blows from swords or lances on the battlefield. His squire helped him to put the armour on, and to look after it.

Underclothes

The knights were the most important soldiers in the castle. A boy of noble birth could begin training as a knight at about the age of seven. He first became a page and learned obedience and manners. At 14 he became a squire and worked for a knight. The knight taught him all the skills he would need in battle. A squire was finally made a knight at a dubbing ceremony, where he was touched on each shoulder with a sword.

Lance

High saddle

Jousting was a popular sport for knights and good training for battle. Two knights would charge towards each other on horseback. Each knight had to try to knock the other one off his horse by hitting him with a lance.

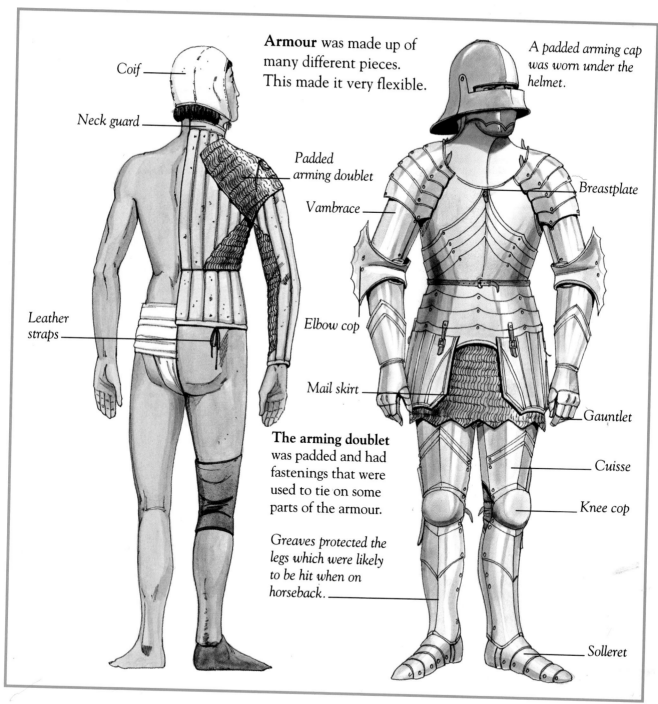

Coif

Neck guard

Armour was made up of many different pieces. This made it very flexible.

A *padded arming cap was worn under the helmet.*

Padded arming doublet

Vambrace

Breastplate

Elbow cop

Leather straps

Mail skirt

Gauntlet

Cuisse

The arming doublet was padded and had fastenings that were used to tie on some parts of the armour.

Knee cop

Greaves protected the legs which were likely to be hit when on horseback.

Solleret

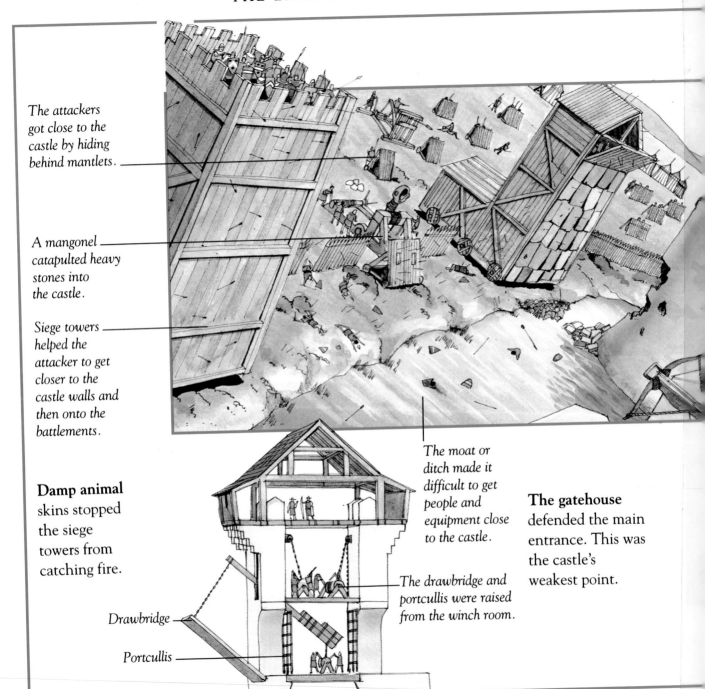

The attackers got close to the castle by hiding behind mantlets.

A mangonel catapulted heavy stones into the castle.

Siege towers helped the attacker to get closer to the castle walls and then onto the battlements.

Damp animal skins stopped the siege towers from catching fire.

The moat or ditch made it difficult to get people and equipment close to the castle.

The gatehouse defended the main entrance. This was the castle's weakest point.

The drawbridge and portcullis were raised from the winch room.

Drawbridge

Portcullis

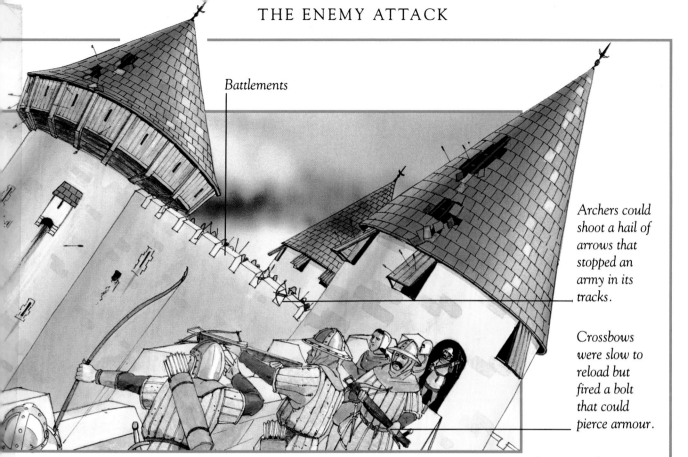

Battlements

Archers could shoot a hail of arrows that stopped an army in its tracks.

Crossbows were slow to reload but fired a bolt that could pierce armour.

When the enemy attacked,

the drawbridge was raised and the castle inhabitants prepared for battle. Soldiers lined the battlements. Because the castle was so difficult to get into, the attackers needed special weapons to help them break through the walls.

A siege could be long and bloody. Many soldiers of both sides would die.

— *Knights prepared for battle.*

It was essential to have a water supply within the castle walls, so that it could not be poisoned by the enemy.

— *The injured had their wounds treated.*

Enemy soldiers tried to make a weak point in the castle. Then they attacked.

The enemy sometimes crossed the moat in boats.

Foot soldiers

The drawbridge was raised to leave a large gap between the gatehouse and the enemy.

Hoardings were wooden galleries at the top of a wall, where soldiers could attack the enemy below.

A battle for a castle was usually long and hard. A siege could last for months, even a year. This meant that food and drink were just as important as weapons. Hunger and thirst could force a castle to surrender. But over the years, cannons became more and more powerful until no castle could survive bombardment for long. This meant that castles became less important.

Cannons fired a large stone or a metal ball that could smash a hole in a castle wall.

A carving in Rome shows an early fortified building called a castrum. The word 'castle' comes from this.

Peñafiel Castle in Spain was built in a good defensive position high on a hilltop. This gave a good view of any approaching enemy.

All over the world

people have built castles as fortresses and homes. Although they were all designed to protect their owners from enemy armies, they are very different too. In recent times, however, rich and powerful people have built castles to show off their power. Castles no longer have any military importance.

Windsor Castle belongs to the British royal family. It is one of the few castles still used as a home.

Castel del Monte in Italy has eight sides. It has a tower at each corner which is octagonal too.

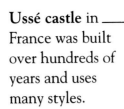

Ussé castle in France was built over hundreds of years and uses many styles.

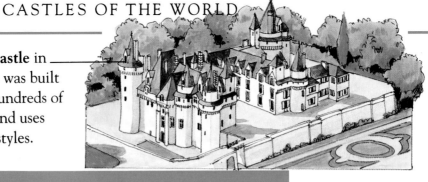

The White Tower is the oldest part of the Tower of London.

The Crusaders built castles like Krak des Chevaliers, when they were fighting in the Holy Land.

Neuschwanstein castle in Germany looks like a castle from the Middle Ages. In fact it was built hundreds of years later, in the 19th century.

The palace at Amber was also a fort. It was built in India in the 17th century.

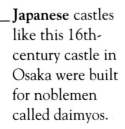

Japanese castles like this 16th-century castle in Osaka were built for noblemen called daimyos.

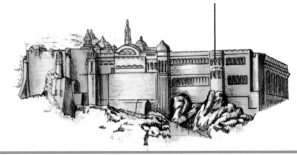

USEFUL WORDS

Barbican A tower that protected the outer gate.

Barracks A building where soldiers live.

Battlements Castle walls with gaps in the top for soldiers to fire through.

Bombardment A non-stop attack with cannons.

Crusades The wars between the Christian and the Muslim armies that started in the 11th century in the Holy Land.

Drawbridge A bridge that could be raised or moved to leave a gap over a ditch.

Dungeon An underground room where prisoners were kept.

Fortress A place to defend the people inside.

Gatehouse A tower built to defend an entrance.

Holy Land Today this is the area of Israel, Jordan and Syria.

Lance A long, sharp pole used as a weapon to knock men off their horses.

Mantlet A large wooden shield that soldiers could move around in battle.

Medieval From the Middle Ages.

Missile Something that is thrown or shot through the air.

Normans People from Normandy, in the north of France.

Portcullis A gate made of wood and metal that could be raised and lowered.

Ramparts Walls used to defend a castle or a town.

Smithy The workshop, or forge, of a smith. A smith is someone who makes things, usually with metals.

Solar A room in the upper part of a castle.